DELUXE Fiddling Method

by Craig Duncan

Online Audio & Video

Audio
www.melbay.com/93742BCDEB
Video
dv.melbay.com/93742
You Tube
www.melbay.com/93742V

This book has appeared in past print runs with a different cover design and photograph. The contents remain the same.

Cover photo courtesy of Lydia Light, photographer.

AUDIO CONTENTS

1	Introduction (:13)
2	Bile Them Cabbage Down/Page 22 (1:13)
3	Bile Them Cabbage Down/Page 23 (1:10)
4	Bile Them Cabbage Down/Page 22 (:37)
5	Bile Them Cabbage Down/Page 23 (:39)
6	Cripple Creek/Page 25 (1:11)
7	Cripple Creek/Page 25 (:40)
8	Old Joe Clark/Page 26 (3:14)
9	Old Joe Clark//Page 26 (1:43)
10	Jenny Lind/Page 28 (1:44)
11	Jenny Lind/Page 28 (1:02)
12	Ida Red/Page 30 (1:13)
13	Ida Red/Page 30 (:38)
14	The Slide/Page 30 (:46)
15	Devil's Dream/Page 32 (1:10)
16	Devil's Dream/Page 32 (:41)
17	Endings/Page 34 (1:51)
18	Eighth of January/Page 38 (1:42)
19	Mississippi Sawyer/Page 39 (1:53)
20	Soldier's Joy/Page 40 (1:51)
21	Liberty/Page 41 (1:54)
22	Chicken Reel/Page 42 (1:02)
23	Rachel/Page 43 (1:11)
24	Rachel/Page 43 (:42)
25	Fisher's Hornpipe/Page 44 (2:47)
26	Forked Deer/Page 45 (1:54)
27	St. Ann's Reel/Page 47 (1:55)
28	Arkansas Traveler/Page 48 (3:28)
29	Arkansas Traveler/Page 48 (1:55)
30	Golden Slippers/Page 52 (1:52)
31	Liza Jane/Page 53 (1:02)
32	Liza Jane/Page 53 (:51)
33	Goodbye Liza Jane/Page 54 (1:21)
34	Red Wing/Page 55 (:44)
35	Turkey in the Straw/Page 56 (:41)
36	Irish Washerwoman/Page 57 (:39)
37	Flowers of Edinburgh/Page 59 (1:37)
38	Blackberry Blossom/Page 60 (1:41)
39	Blackberry Blossom Variations/Page 60 (:56)
40	Bully of the Town/Page 62 (1:00)
41	Down Yonder/Page 64 (:45)
42	Stone's Rag/Page 69 (:51)
43	I Don't Love Nobody/Page 70 (:30)
44	Billy in the Low Ground/Page 71 (:38)
45	East Tennessee Blues/Page 72 (:41)
46	Tennessee Wagneer/Page 74 (:59)
47	Back up and Push/Page 75 (:36)
48	Back Up and Push/Page 76 (:39)
49	Rose of Sharon/Page 79 (1:41)
50	Westphalia Waltz/Page 80 (1:35)
51	Over the Waves/Page 82 (1:38)
52	Golden Anniversary/Page 85 (1:08)
53	Cottoneyed Joe-Western/Page 92 (1:02)
54	Cottoneyed Joe-Eastern/Page 93 (:39)

Also Available: *Advanced Fiddling*

1 2 3 4 5 6 7 8 9 0

Visit us on the Web at www.melbay.com — E-mail us at email@melbay.com

Table of Contents

About The Author

Craig Duncan is an active Nashville musician who spans the gap of both the country and classical music fields. He began playing the violin at the age of eight and went on to receive a Bachelor of Music degree from Appalachian State University in Boone, North Carolina. He began his professional music career in Charlotte, North Carolina where he worked as fiddler, vocalist and bassist. After moving to Nashville, Craig began working as a fiddler and vocalist at Opryland, U.S.A. with a group called Smoky Mountain Sunshine. In addition to performing at Opryland, this group did shows such as the Porter Wagoner Show, the Canadian National Exhibition in Toronto, Canada, and various conventions throughout the country. In September of 1978 Craig went to work on the Grand Ole Opry with Wilma Lee Cooper, as fiddler and vocalist. He performed weekly on the Opry and did TV specials such as the Grand Ole Opry TV Special, the Bluegrass Spectacular with Tom T. Hall, and Good 'N Country with Jean Shepard and Justin Tubb. Also during this time he began working with a string section in Nashville doing commercial recordings and performing in A.F. of M. orchestras throughout the Nashville area. Craig went back to work for Opryland in 1980, performing with a contemporary country group. Along with his performance activities, Craig is also Artist/Teacher of Fiddle at the Blair School of Music in Nashville, Tennessee. He is actively involved in carrying on the tradition of American fiddling and is engaged in research, writing and teaching in this field.

Special thanks go to Mark Barnett, Earl Spielman and also to the many people who have allowed the use of their photographs in this book. I dedicate the book to my wife, Susan, for her many hours of typing, editing and assistance in completing this project.

Craig Duncan

FRONT

SIDE

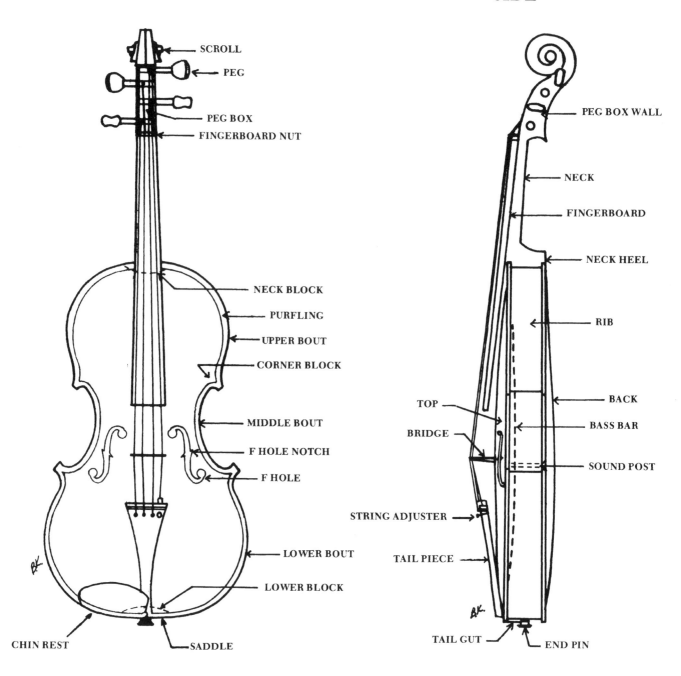

- SCROLL
- PEG
- PEG BOX
- FINGERBOARD NUT
- NECK BLOCK
- PURFLING
- UPPER BOUT
- CORNER BLOCK
- MIDDLE BOUT
- F HOLE NOTCH
- F HOLE
- LOWER BOUT
- LOWER BLOCK
- CHIN REST
- SADDLE

- PEG BOX WALL
- NECK
- FINGERBOARD
- NECK HEEL
- RIB
- TOP
- BACK
- BASS BAR
- BRIDGE
- SOUND POST
- STRING ADJUSTER
- TAIL PIECE
- TAIL GUT
- END PIN

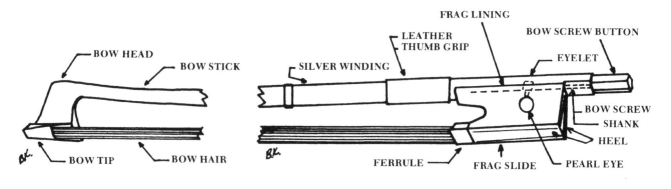

- BOW HEAD
- BOW STICK
- BOW TIP
- BOW HAIR

- FRAG LINING
- LEATHER THUMB GRIP
- BOW SCREW BUTTON
- SILVER WINDING
- EYELET
- BOW SCREW
- SHANK
- HEEL
- FERRULE
- FRAG SLIDE
- PEARL EYE

BOW TIP

BOW FROG

Introduction

This book was written to present a general survey of American fiddling. Its intent is to present the basics of fiddling by beginning with essential bowings and fingerings, and progressing from simple to more advanced renditions of tunes. It should be noted that the tunes included here are only renditions rather than exact statements of the tunes themselves. The aural tradition of fiddling does not allow itself to be pinpointed to one exact transcription of a tune being "the" correct version. Fiddlers from different parts of the country play a given tune in many ways. There are also cases in which the same name is used for two or more tunes. Therefore, to attempt to print the exact melody of a tune would be ludicrous. The tunes here are renditions which the author has played or has heard played by amateur and professional fiddlers. The author has attempted to present usable fingerings, bowings and explanations of each of the tunes covered. For those students of fiddling who do not read music, a very brief discussion of musical notation is included. This discussion would prove more useful if it were supplemented by a book or books specifically designed to explain musical notation. Fiddling is a great part of our musical heritage and it is the author's desire that this heritage continue to grow and flourish. May this book prove successful toward that end.

The History of Fiddling[1]

The first fiddler in America of which we have record was John Utie of England, who sailed up the James River in 1620 on the *Francis Bonaventure*.[2] He was a professional fiddler before sailing for America.

The fiddle became a popular instrument in the British Isles during the sixteenth century, although the earliest record of payment to fiddlers for entertainment took place in the late 1400's. Popular music of the seventeenth and eighteenth centuries in the British Isles was intended for the fiddle or bagpipes. In Scotland and Ireland jigs, reels, clogs, hornpipes, highland flings and pastoral airs were performed prior to the seventeenth century. By the end of the seventeenth century, the fiddle was becoming the predominant instrument.[3]

In the United States and Canada, styles from England, Scotland and Ireland as well as other European traditions began to mingle. Throughout the seventeenth, eighteenth, and nineteenth centuries the fiddle was dominant in folk music. It was light and easy to transport so it was present at social gatherings. The fiddler became the center of community activities as he played at barn raisings, ice cream suppers, husking bees, weddings, wakes and other social events.

[1]The section on the History of Fiddling has been derived from Chapter IV of the doctoral dissertation, *Traditional North American Fiddling*, by Earl V. Spielman, University of Wisconsin-Madison, 1975. The section is included here with permission of Dr. Spielman.

[2]Minutes of the Council and General Court in *Virginia Magazine of History and Biography*, Vol. 19 (1911), pp. 374-376, as cited in Maurer Maurer's article, "The 'Professor of Musick' in Colonial America," *The Musical Quarterly*, Vol. 36, no. 4 (October, 1950), p. 511.

[3]Discussions of the development of the "fiddle" and its acceptance into Scottish music can be found in Francis Collinson, *The Traditional and National Music of Scotland*, Nashville, Vanderbilt University Press, 1966, pp. 199-204, and David Johnson, *Music and Society in Lowland Scotland in the Eighteenth Century*, London, Oxford University Press, 1972, pp. 95-129.

The primary function of fiddling and fiddle music in America prior to the twentieth century, however, has been for dancing. Often the fiddler not only had the responsibility of furnishing the music, but was also responsible for "calling" a dance.[4] Traveling fiddlers would support themselves by moving from community to community playing for dances and other special occasions. They were usually paid by whatever gratuities the community would supply. The fiddler held a position of honor and respect in many communities.[5]

In the late nineteenth century, fiddlers became a part of minstrel shows and were generally featured in combination with banjo, tambourine and bones. The tunes they played were referred to as "jigs," although they had no relation to the term "jig" as a song form. When radio came into use, fiddling found its way onto the airways. On September 9, 1922, "Fiddlin'" John Carson was the first fiddler to play on radio.[6]

The first recordings of fiddle music were done for RCA in the summer of 1922 when Eck Robertson and Henry Gilliland recorded "Sally Gooden" and "Arkansas Traveler" in New York City. These tunes were released on September 1, 1922.[7] The first fiddler to become a commercial success was "Fiddlin'" John Carson on the Okeh label in 1923. This was probably due to his success as a radio performer.

[4]S. Foster Damon, "The History of Square-Dancing," *American Antiquarian Society,* Proceedings at the Annual Meeting. Vol. 62, no. 1 (April 16, 1952), p. 81.

[5]John Q. Wolf, "A Country Dance in the Ozarks in 1874," *Southern Folklore Quarterly,* Vol. 29, no. 4 (December, 1965), p. 319.

[6]"Radio Made 'Fiddlin' John Carson Famous," *Radio Digest,* November 7, 1925.

[7]Victor No. 18956. See also Stephen F. Davis, "A. C. (Eck) Robertson Discography," *The Devil's Box,* Tennessee Valley Old Time Fiddlers Association newsletter, No. 17 (June 1, 1972), pp. 17-19. See also Bill C. Malone, *Country Music U.S.A.,* Austin, University of Texas Press, 1968.

On April 19, 1924, WLS Chicago began the first important "hillbilly" or country music show featuring fiddle tunes, comedy and square dancing. In October of 1925, WSM Nashville began broadcasting the Grand Ole Opry which has become the longest running country music radio show.

Because of radio and recordings, country music became more refined and singing began to be emphasized rather than fiddling. As a result, the fiddle became part of a band and was used more and more to back up singers and other instruments as well as to play lead. Professional musicians developed out of this period and fiddling became more refined and planned with definite arrangements. The appearance of fiddle records caused other fiddlers to learn new tunes and arrangements. The recordings also caused the public to expect more of the local fiddler. By the 1930's, the fiddle had taken a back seat to the voice. Some of the important string bands of the time were Gid Tanner and the Skillet Lickers, J. E. Mainer and his Mountaineers, and Charlie Poole and the North Carolina Ramblers.

Western Swing, beginning in the 1930's, became another important musical development which included (and expanded the style of) the fiddle. Bob Wills and the Texas Playboys used fiddles to perform the "swing" music of the day, and incorporated some traditional fiddle music performed with a "swing" accompaniment.

In the 1940's, bluegrass emerged as a style in which the fiddle plays an extremely important part. This style of music has grown in popularity over the past decades and has helped to maintain a traditional sound in fiddle music.

Fiddle music is more polished and refined today than ever. The fiddle has developed from an instrument used as the sole lead to one used for lead, back-up and rhythm.

Many fiddle organizations have been developed over the past few years to preserve traditional fiddling, as is evidenced by the many Old-Time Fiddlers conventions and contests. Fiddle contests seem to have always been popular in America. The first recorded contest was held in Hanover County, Virginia on November 30, 1736, for which the first prize was "a fine Cremona Fiddle."[8] Although this is the first contest on record, there were probably other contests taking place in this time period. References to contests can be found throughout the 1800's and 1900's and have grown extremely popular within the last generation. Fiddle contests now number in the hundreds each year and can be found in practically every state. The popularity of contests today is strong evidence of their entertainment (and commercial) value, yet they are equally important in preserving an art form and a body of music so important in American history. Fiddling is a strong part of the American heritage, and will undoubtedly continue to thrive and develop in the generations to come.

Fiddlin' John Carson

Eck Robertson

Photograph courtesy of the Country Music Foundation Library and Media Center, Nashville, Tennessee

[8]Richard Hulan, "The First Annual County Fiddlers Contest," *The Devil's Box*, Tennessee Valley Old Time Fiddlers Association newsletter, No. 13 (March 15, 1969), pp. 15-18.

Overview of Musical Notation

For the purpose of this book, two aspects of reading music will be discussed, pitch and rhythm. The staff and clef signs were developed to represent pitch. The staff consists of five lines and four spaces. The clef determines what pitches the lines and spaces represent. Pitches have an alphabetical name from A through G. After G, the naming process repeats itself. Fiddle music is written in treble clef (or G clef), which determines that the second line from the bottom is G above middle C.

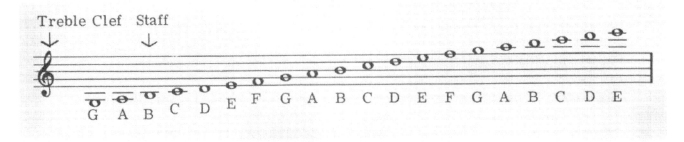

The distance between each letter name or pitch is a whole step except between B and C, and between E and F. These are half steps.

Sharps and flats may be added to change the relationship of the whole and half steps. A sharp (♯) raises a pitch by a half step and a flat (♭) lowers a pitch by a half step. A natural sign (♮) negates flats and sharps, returning the pitch to its original state.

The key signature is indicated at the beginning of the staff following the clef sign. It indicates which notes are to be flatted or sharped, if any. When a flat or sharp is found in the key signature, it indicates that all pitches bearing the same name as the indicated pitch are to be altered by the flat or sharp.

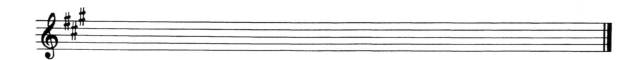

In the key signature found above, three pitches are sharped. The first is F♯, meaning all F's become F♯'s. The second is C♯, meaning all C's become C♯'s, and the third is G♯, meaning all G's become G♯'s. This key signature indicates the key of A, for which a given set of finger patterns is to be used. Each key revolves around the note of its name; for example, the key of A revolves around A, the key of D around D, etc. It is always important to look at the key signatures so that you will know what key to play in and which notes to flat or sharp.

The symbols for note values have a direct relationship to each other, and create the rhythm of the piece. Likewise, the symbols for rest values have the same relationship. The following diagrams illustrate these relationships.

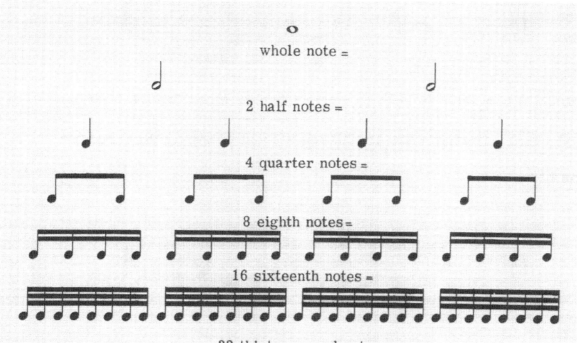

whole note =

2 half notes =

4 quarter notes =

8 eighth notes =

16 sixteenth notes =

32 thirty-second notes

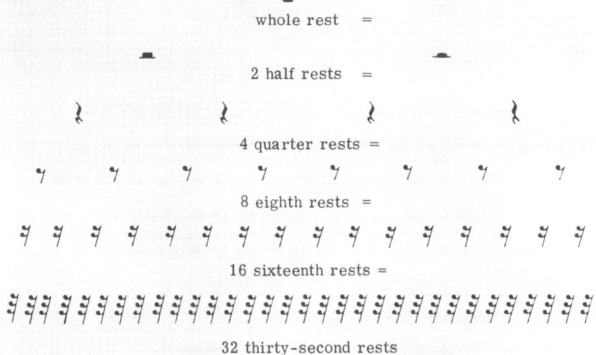

whole rest =

2 half rests =

4 quarter rests =

8 eighth rests =

16 sixteenth rests =

32 thirty-second rests

Adding a dot after a note increases it by one-half its original value.

Therefore

When two notes on the same pitch are connected by a tie (⌣), the length

of the two notes is added and played as one note.

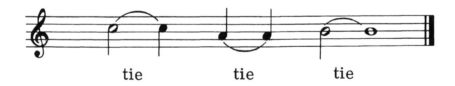

tie   tie   tie

When this symbol is used to connect two or more different pitches, it is

called a slur, and the notes are played without changing the direction

of the bow.

slur   slur

Bowing

There are two bow directions. Down-bow is the movement of the bow across the strings from the frog to the tip. It is indicated by this sign (⊓). Up-bow is the movement of the bow across the strings from the tip to the frog, and is indicated by this sign (V).

The time signature follows the key signature on the first line of the tune. It indicates how many beats are in a measure and what note receives the beat.

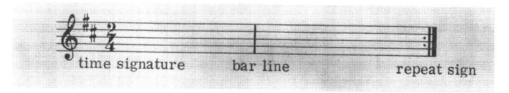

time signature   bar line   repeat sign

Many fiddle tunes are written in $\frac{2}{4}$. This time signature indicates two beats per measure, with the quarter note equaling one beat. Each group of two beats is separated by a bar line. The measure includes those notes within the bar lines. The length of the measure is indicated by the time signature. A repeat sign is often found at the end of a section. It means to go back to the previous repeat sign or if no other exists, then to the beginning, and play the section over. Often in fiddle tunes, first and second endings are used. This is illustrated in the following example:

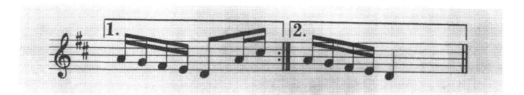

When playing a section using first and second endings, play the first ending the first time and the second ending the second time.

Holding the Fiddle

There are many possible ways to hold the fiddle, from the old-time fiddler who supports it against his side to the concert violinist who holds it in a very formal position. The following method of holding the instrument is presented as a guideline in developing a position which is comfortable and allows the easiest approach to fiddling.

The fiddle is held between the chin and the collarbone. By supporting the instrument entirely with the chin and shoulder, the left hand is free to carry out its function of determining the various notes and is not required to hold the instrument. There are many types of shoulder rests available, and many fiddlers find it more comfortable to use one. It is recommended that the student experiment with and without a shoulder rest to find the most comfortable and efficient way to hold the instrument.

The fiddle should be held to the left side rather than in front, with the left arm and elbow held underneath. The only parts of the left hand which should touch the instrument are the thumb and the index finger. The palm should not come in contact with the neck. The placement of the hand, in relation to the fingerboard should be determined by the size of the hand, depending on what position will allow the fingertips to most easily touch the fingerboard. The fingers should come from above the instrument so that it is possible for the fingertips to touch one string at a time. Do not grip the neck of the fiddle, as this creates tension and the left hand should be as relaxed as possible. Always use the tips of the fingers, never allowing them to lay flat. The wrist should be held in a straight line with the knuckles and the forearm. This position will allow the best possible use of the left hand with the least possible effort.

Holding the Bow

The way the bow is held will change with the various aspects of playing. The grip shifts slightly as the bow moves across the strings and as different volume levels and tone qualities are utilized. The basic grip presented here permits the flexibility of the hand to develop and should be practiced until it becomes a natural position.

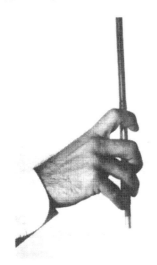 

The first finger should touch the bow between the first and second joints. The middle and ring fingers should wrap around the bow comfortably and the tip of the little finger should rest on the top edge of the bow. The fingers should be curved and spread apart. The thumb should be placed partially on the frog and partially on the stick, forming a circle with the middle finger. Always bend the thumb outward as this eliminates excess tension in the right hand. The bow should be held with as little pressure as possible.

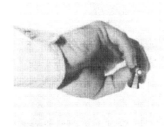 

Using the Bow

The names of the open strings, from highest to lowest in pitch are

E - A -D - G. They are notated on the following spaces of the treble clef. Use

of the bow should begin on the open strings.

The bow should be placed on the string parallel to the bridge, form-

ing a right angle with the strings. It should be midway between

the bridge and the fingerboard and drawn with a straight stroke. The

wrist and elbow should bend together to allow the bow to move straight.

The right shoulder should be completely relaxed and should remain relaxed

in all phases of bowing. The shoulder should never be raised. When the

bow is placed on the string in the middle portion of the bow, the elbow

should be approximately the same height as the bow, in a rather straight

line with the wrist. This creates the least amount of tension in the right

arm as well as making for the most efficient placement of the arm. Shorter

players can more easily use the entire length of the bow if they swing the

scroll more toward the front than toward the left side.

There are three main things which affect the sound produced by the bow:

sounding point, or placement of the bow in relation to the bridge,

pressure and speed. Placing the bow nearer the bridge produces a louder

and more cutting sound, and positioning the bow nearer the fingerboard pro-

duces a softer, more muted sound. Less pressure produces less sound and more pressure produces more sound. The slower the bow speed, the softer the sound; the faster the bow speed, the louder the sound.

As a general rule, the beginning student should use the following combination of these factors: The bow should be placed midway between the fingerboard and bridge, never going over the fingerboard. The cleanest, most cutting or carrying sound is about 1/4 inch from the bridge. This may sound harsh to the ear, but will cause the sound to project from the fiddle. Allow the weight of the bow to produce the sound, rather than applying extra pressure with the hand and/or arm. As the bow nears the tip, the wrist should be turned inward so that the pressure remains constant throughout the stroke. As the weight of the bow is greater near the frog, less pressure should be used in that area of the bow. Too much pressure will cause the strings to produce a scratchy sound. The student should use as much bow speed as the music will allow; in other words, use as much bow as possible. From the beginning, the student should practice using long, full bow strokes. Make certain the bow is drawn perfectly straight; otherwise, it will "travel" up and down the strings and produce an unpleasant sound. The bow should be tilted slightly outward so that the hair faces the bridge. This gives a cleaner, sharper sound than a perfectly flat bow.

The height of the right elbow should determine which string is being played. On the G string, the elbow is high, on the D string it is a little lower, on the A string it is a little lower yet, and on the E string, the elbow is held down to the side. Double stops (two strings at once) are performed by playing with equal bow pressure on two strings. Elbow placement should be half-way between the placement for the two individual strings. Thus seven positions exist — one for each open string, and one for each set of two strings.

Elbow Placement — G String

Elbow Placement — D String

Elbow Placement — A String

Elbow Placement — E String

String crossings should be done with as little movement as possible so that the smoothest sound is produced. In fast passages such as in Devil's Dream (see page 32), the elbow is placed so that two strings are easily accessible and the string crossing is done with the wrist and forearm.

Key of A

The key of A has three sharps, F♯, C♯ and G♯ which are notated at the beginning of the staff like this:

When these sharps are present, it means that all F's, C's and G's in the piece are sharps, unless otherwise notated.

The finger pattern or spacing used in the key of A is the same for the A and E strings. The first finger is placed about an inch from the nut (the end of the fingerboard), the second finger about an inch from the first finger, the third finger next to the second finger, possibly touching it (depending on the hand size), and the fourth finger about three-fourths of an inch higher.

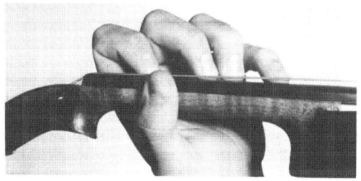

Here is a diagram of the notes on the A and E strings:

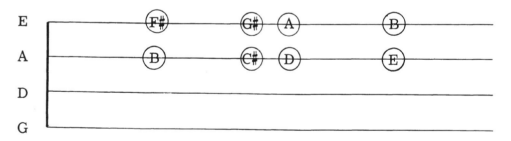

Practice playing the notes in a scale starting on open A string, first finger on the A string, second finger, third finger; then open E, and first, second and third fingers on the E string. The notes are written on the staff like this:

20

Notice that the fourth finger on the A string and the open E string should sound the same pitch. You should learn to play the note both ways. Practice the scale using long bow strokes until you are comfortable with the placement of the fingers and can produce a nice sound.

Fiddlers use a bowing pattern that is often referred to as a shuffle. It consists of three strokes which are continually repeated. Start with a long down-bow, then a short up-bow, followed by a short down-bow. The pattern is then repeated using opposite bowings - long up-bow, short down-bow, and short up-bow. The long note is exactly twice as long as the short note. This bowing pattern can be written any of the following ways:

Notice that the pattern is the relationship of a long note followed by two short notes, regardless of the way it is written. For the purposes of this book, it will usually be written as an eighth followed by two sixteenths. Ex.

Practice the pattern on the open strings. When you are comfortable with that,you should try it on the A scale like this:

21

This is the most important bowing pattern you will learn so you should practice it with care, making sure you keep a constant, steady beat and that the first note in the shuffle is twice as long as each of the other notes. Now that you know the A scale and the shuffle bowing, you are ready for your first fiddle tune.

Bile Them Cabbage Down

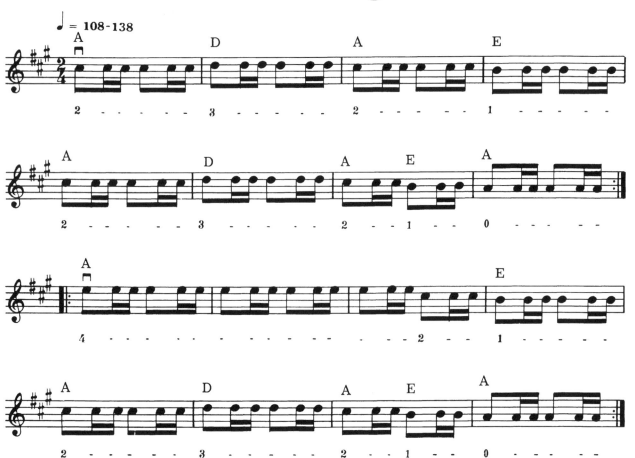

Make sure you are playing in tune and the bowing is staying steady and exact. Practice slowly at first and speed up gradually as you are more comfortable with the tune.

You can add to the tune by playing two strings at the same time. This is referred to as using a drone or double stops. Play the tune exactly as you did before, but this time play both the E and the A strings together, making certain not to let the fingers touch the E string.

Roy Acuff and the Smoky Mountain Boys.
From left: Onie Wheeler, Gene Martin, Roy Acuff,
Charlie Collins and Oswald Kirby

One change will have to be made - when you are playing the third finger D on the A string, you should play first finger F♯ on the E string at the same time. In the beginning of the second part, the fourth finger should sound the same pitch as the open E string and both should be played together.

Bile Them Cabbage Down

Kathy Kuhn and Steven Springer

We are now ready to add the A scale on the G and D strings. Here is a diagram of the finger pattern on these two strings:

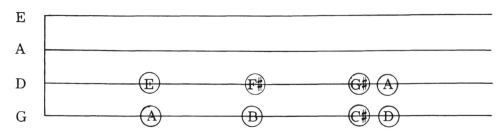

You will notice that the third finger has been moved up so that it touches the fourth finger instead of the second finger, thus making a whole step between the second and third fingers and a half step between the third and fourth fingers.

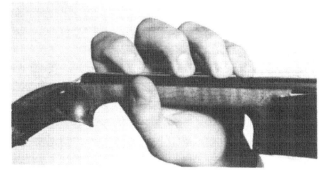

The notes are written on the staff like this:

When you have learned this scale, put the two together to form a two octave A major scale.

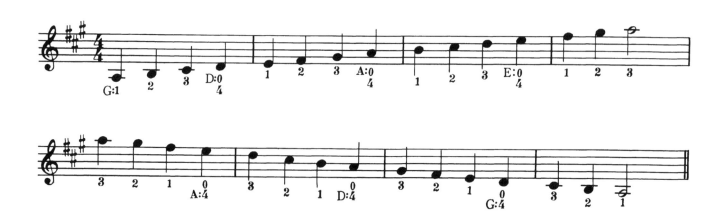

24

Cripple Creek

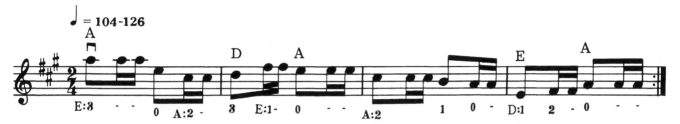

This is the simple melody in the key of A, using the shuffle bowing. We can make the tune fancier by embellishing (adding to) the melody. This is often done by fiddlers. Take special care to keep the shuffle bowing going. When you see a slur (⌒), play the notes within the slur in one bow stroke.

Tater Tate

25

Old Joe Clark

This is the basic melody line of Old Joe Clark using the shuffle bowing. Notice the natural sign (♮). This cancels the G♯, meaning that the second finger G on the E string is played low, or touching the first finger. Also the third finger G on the D string is played low next to the second finger when the natural sign is present. Note: Be very careful to keep the second finger high on the A string and low on the E.

A simple variation is to play the same notes while bowing two strings. When fingering either on the A or the E string, bow the A and E strings together. When fingering on the D string, the D and A strings are bowed. It is necessary to add the first finger on the A string in the fourth measure of each part so that the correct chord is sounded.

Benny Martin

26

Here is an embellished version of Old Joe Clark, created by adding notes around the melody. Be certain to observe the bow markings so that the shuffle bowing continues throughout the tune.

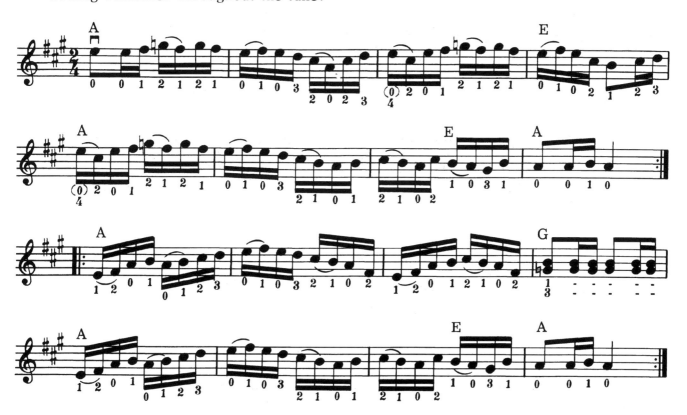

Jenny Lind

The first part of this tune does not stay with the shuffle bowing; rather, the bowing is adjusted to fit the tune. The second part uses the shuffle bowing throughout except where the notes are held out. Use the fourth finger for the E's, because it will be necessary to do so for the following doubling:

Notice that the fourth finger E on the A string and the open E are to be played together. This is very common in fiddling. You will also notice that the ending has been embellished by adding a triplet (three notes played on a beat or division of a beat). Long bow strokes should be used on this tune to give it a smooth, flowing sound.

The Slide

The slide is a technique commonly used by fiddlers, of which there are several types. Four of the more common slides are: 1) starting a note flat and sliding up to the pitch, 2) starting on the pitch and sliding down to flatten the pitch, 3) starting on the pitch, sliding flat, and returning to the pitch, and 4) starting flat, going up to the pitch, and sliding flat again. As a general rule, a slide should never go sharp. Slides of more than a half step will sound over exaggerated except for those instances where the slide is used in the form of a glissando. For practical purposes, the slide should never cover more than a half step. The duration of the slide should be determined by its context.

Two symbols have been used in this book for slides. One is indicated by an arrow in the direction of the slide. The other is a slash mark in the direction of the slide. Examples: 1. ⟋⟍ 2. ⟋⟍

Craig Duncan

Jim and Jesse McReynolds

Ida Red

The first type of slide may be used in the first two measures of the tune. Begin the notated C♯ as a C♮ and slide up to the C♯.

The same passage may be played using the second type of slide by beginning on the C♯ and sliding downward.

The third type of slide may be played in the same passage by beginning on the C♯, sliding downward to the C♮ and back up to the C♯.

The fourth type of slide may also be used in this passage by beginning on a C♮, sliding up to the C♯ and back down to the C♮.

Practice the slides until you have control and can land exactly on the right pitch. Three important points to remember about slides are:

1. Keep the slide within a half-step.

2. Slide to or from a definite pitch;
   do not slide at random.

3. Do not overuse the slide.

Slides and drones may also be combined in playing Ida Red. Be certain to only slide on one string so that the drone remains constant.

Randy Howard   *Buddy Spicher and Benny Martin*

Devil's Dream

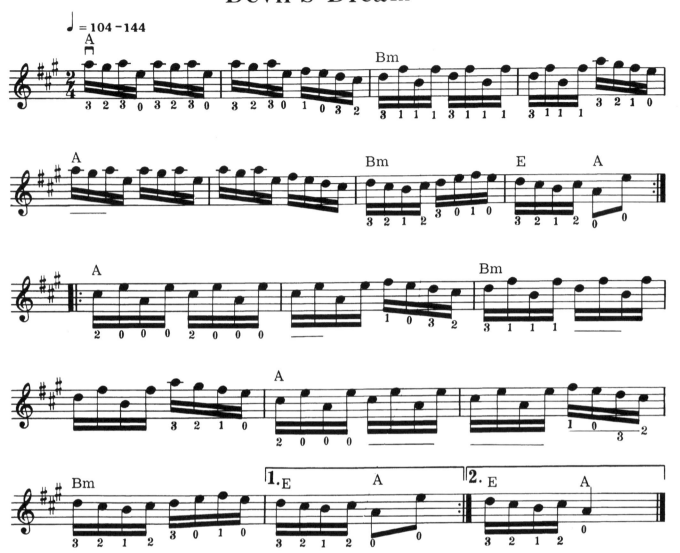

This is an old standard fiddle tune. The bowing of this tune should be done with all separate strokes. This will allow you to do the "rocking" type bowing that is required in measures 3 and 4. Try to use as little movement as possible with the right arm, allowing the bow to rock only enough to sound clearly on each string. The right hand will make a circular motion when the bowing is done correctly. Practice the bowing slowly on open strings, gradually increasing the speed, until you are comfortable with it.

Now try it with the fingerings. For measures 3 and 4 (and other occurences of the same notes), the first finger should touch both the E and the A strings so that the third finger is the only one moved.

Mark O'Conner

Clayton "Pappy" McMichen

Photographs courtesy of the Country Music
Foundation Library and Media Center,
Nashville, Tennessee

Buddy Spicher, Red Taylor and Dale Potter

Endings

At the completion of a fiddle tune a tag or ending is usually added to let the listener and accompanying musicians know the tune is over. The ending is normally four beats long, but is often doubled to eight beats. One of the most popular endings of all is the "shave and a haircut" ending. It can be played single or double string and is the basis for many other endings.

Examples of use of the "shave and a haircut" ending:

Another common ending is based on a descending scale. Here are a few examples of the many possible variations.

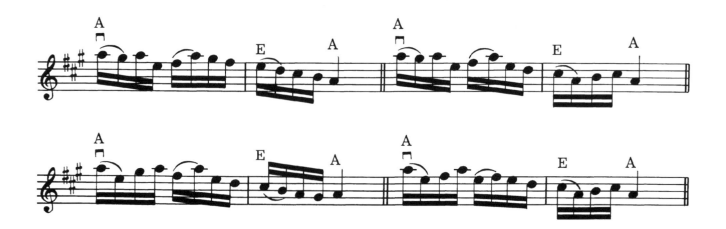

These endings may be combined to form a double ending such as in the following example.

By moving the endings across one string, beginning on the A string instead of the E string, they are transposed to the key of D. By moving over one more string and beginning on the D string, they are transposed to the key of G.

Key of D

Key of G

The endings presented here are only a few of the many possibilities. Through listening to fiddle music, many more endings will be discovered and put to use by the creative fiddler.

Key of D

The key of D has two sharps, F♯ and C♯. They are notated at the beginning of the staff like this:

There are three different finger patterns used in this key; one for the E string, one for the A and the D strings, and one for the G string. The pattern on the E string should look like this:

Notice the closeness of the first and second fingers. In the pattern used for both the D and the A strings, the second finger is moved up to touch the third finger.

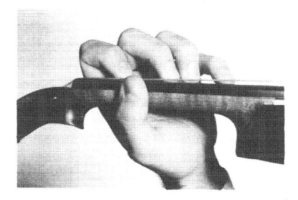

The finger pattern for the G string has high second and third fingers. Notice that the third and fourth fingers are touching.

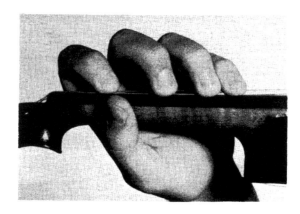

Here is a diagram of the notes in the key of D.

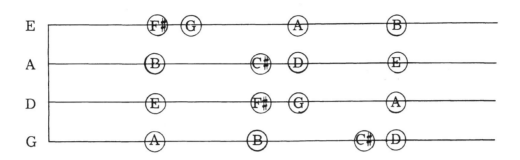

The corresponding notes on the staff are written like this:

Be certain to observe the key signature so that you will know which notes are sharped.

The Misty Mountain Boys
From left: Craig Duncan, John Rumble, Gordon
Reid, Pete Corum and Jay Grizzle

Eighth of January

This is an old fiddle tune that was used by Johnny Horton in his song "The Battle of New Orleans." It may be approached many different ways. The second part is often played down an octave. Be certain to use the fourth finger to bring out the melody and to strengthen the drone sound.

These parts may be combined to form further variations of your own. The main thing to keep in mind is to be able to hear the melody in whatever variations you may play.

This variation may also be played with a drone A string.

Mississippi Sawyer

This is a good standard fiddle tune that emphasizes the shuffle bowing. It should not be played too fast, but rather with a good bounce to it.

The Bluegrass Cardinals with Tim Smith on the fiddle

Buddy Spicher

Soldier's Joy

This is an old Scotch-Irish fiddle tune. The beat should be very strong, as the tune is often used for dancing. Using the open A string in the first, third and fifth measures of the first part will help bring out this feeling. It should be noted that the second part is actually an embellishment of the melody. The actual melodic line is very simple:

Liberty

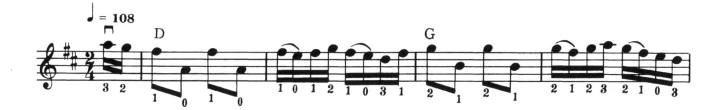

This is another tune which should not be played too fast. Special attention should be given to the dotted eighth sixteenth rhythm (♪. ♪). Make certain that the dotted eighth lasts three-fourths of a beat or the length of three sixteenths.

Bartow Riley

Joe Stuart

Chicken Reel

Once again, we find the slide in this fiddle tune. This slide actually starts a half step flat (on the F♮) and drags up to the F♯. Obviously, the tune is mocking the sound of a chicken cackling and therefore the slide should be exaggerated. The bowing on the second part of the tune should be done with separate strokes. The second measure of this part should be played with the third finger remaining in place on the A string and rocking the bow to the open E and first finger on the E string.

Kenny Baker, Craig Duncan and Blaine Sprouse

Rachel

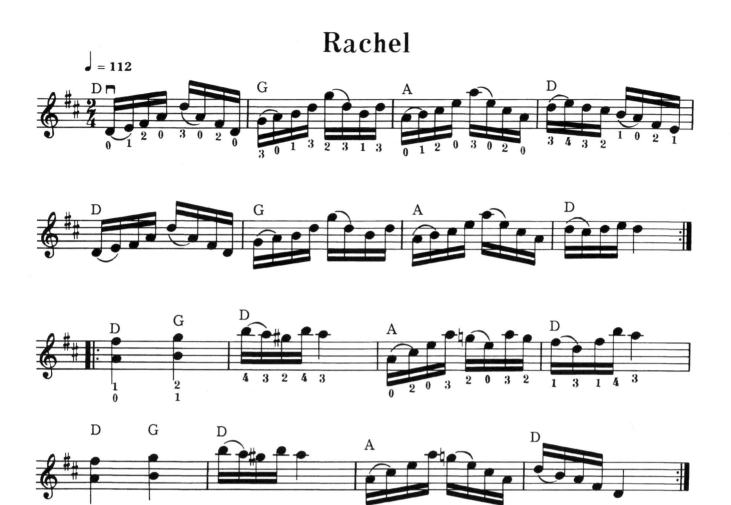

The first part of this tune is very straightforward with the fiddle melody outlining the accompanying chords. The second part introduces a G♯ into the melodic line. A big difference should be made between the G♮'s and G♯'s so that they both sound in tune and correct in their context. The quarter notes in the second part should be played with long, full bow strokes. The first and fifth measures of the second part are often played with an E grace note so that they sound:

These two measures may also be played with the chords inverted like this:

Fisher's Hornpipe

This is a very old tune which was passed down through the generations in the key of F with only two parts. Over the past few years, instrumentalists have begun playing it in D. The third part presented here was used by Eck Robertson in the early 1920's and has become fairly well established as an addition to the tune.

Notice the bowing at the end of the second and third parts. There is an extra slur into the second beat. This is a corrective measure to make the bowing come out downbow for the repeat. This procedure is fairly common and should be mastered for use in other similar situations.

Forked Deer

Once again, we find the need for a corrective bowing to keep the shuffle moving with the down-bow on the downbeat. The second half of beat two in measure 4 should be slurred into the first half of beat one in measure 5. Likewise, the second half of beat two in the first ending should be slurred into the first half of beat one in the first measure of the repeat. By learning this bowing device, awkward bowings can be avoided.

Vernon Soloman

After learning the melody of the second part as it is written above, you should learn to play it with a fourth finger drone. All of the A's will be played with the fourth finger on the D string and the open A string sounding simultaneously. The notes above A are played with the fourth finger down, and the notes below A are played with the open A string sounding while noting on the D string. The next to the last measure is played single string.

Trianon Ballroom
Home of
Bob Wills and His Texas Playboys

Left to right: Eldon Shamblin (guitar), Lucky Moeller, Bob White (fiddle), Tiny Moore (mandolin), unidentified man, Jimmy Widener (tenor banjo), Bob Wills (fiddle), BillyJack Wills (drums), Johnny Gimble (mandolin), unidentified man, Keith Coleman (fiddle), Luke Wills (bass), Mancel Tierney (piano), Herb Remington (steel guitar), John Wills (fiddle).

St. Anne's Reel

St. Anne's Reel is a Scotch-Irish tune that is very popular in Canada. Canadian fiddlers often use trills and grace notes. The thirty-second notes in measures 4 are to be played as a quick trill or grace note. Pay special attention to the C 's in measures 3 and 4. These are to be played with the second finger next to the first finger, using the same finger pattern on the A string as the one on the E string. The second finger then moves back to the original finger pattern for the remainder of the tune. The second beat of measures 9 and 13 should be done with separate bow strokes to make the string crossings cleaner. The bowing then works itself back to the shuffle on the triplets in measures 10 and 14.

Arkansas Traveler

This is a two-part tune with variations. It begins with the doubled fourth finger and open D string, which is used again in measures 2 and 5. Part three is an embellishment of part one, continuing in the double stop, drone style. The last two measures of part three are played identically to the last two measures of part one, with the exception that the bow plays both the D and the A strings. Part four is a variation on part two, which is played down one octave. The next variation, part five, is an embellished melody played in the higher octave without double stops. Part six is a repeat of part two. Although a D chord is implied in the third measures of parts two and four, a G chord is often played. An often used ending for this tune employs the beginning and ending phrases of the tune.

Key of G

The key of G has one sharp, F#. It is notated at the beginning of the staff like this:
this:

There are two finger patterns used in the key of G; one for the G and D strings, and one for the A and E strings. The pattern on the G and D strings is the same as the pattern on the D and A strings in the key of D. It looks like this:

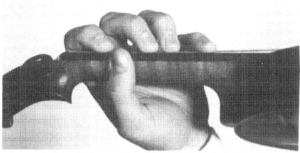

The pattern for the A and E strings in the key of G is the same as it is for the E string in the key of D. It looks like this:

Here is a diagram of the notes in the key of G.

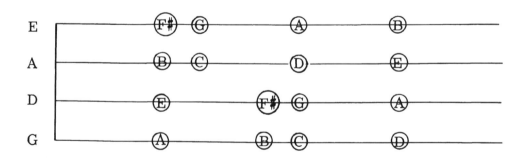

The corresponding notes on the staff are written like this:

Be certain to look at the key signature so that you know which key you are playing in and which finger patterns to use.

Bill Monroe and the Bluegrass Boys: from left, Kenny Baker, Butch Robbins, Bill Monroe, Mark Embry, Wayne Lewis

Golden Slippers

This is an old gospel tune that has become very popular as an instrumental. The words to the chorus are:

> Oh dem Golden Slippers
> Oh dem Golden Slippers
> The Golden Slippers I's goin' to wear
> They goin' to be so neat.
> Oh dem Golden Slippers
> Oh dem Golden Slippers
> The Golden Slippers I's goin' to wear
> On the Golden Streets.

When two fiddlers get together they will often play in harmony with each other. This is called playing "twin" fiddles. Here is a harmony part that can be used as a twin for Golden Slippers.

Liza Jane

Here is an excellent example of taking a simple folk tune and adding to it to create a fiddle tune. As you will notice, the melody is present in the fiddle part and comes through clearly. It is very important when fiddling a tune to make the melody stand out.

Goodbye Liza Jane

This old folk tune is presented with a simple fiddle part and an embellished variation. Once again the original melody is ever present in the variation. The chords in parentheses may be added to give the tune more harmonic color, or they may be omitted. Try to create a part for a simple tune such as Liza Jane, Goodbye Liza Jane, Shortenin' Bread or some other folk tune. Remember to keep the melody in the tune and add or subtract from it for a variation, making certain the melody is heard.

Red Wing

Red Wing is a standard tune played by instrumentalists throughout country and traditional music. The straightforward melody is presented here.

Turkey in the Straw

Turkey in the Straw is possibly one of the most popular of all fiddle tunes. The version presented here is embellished by adding notes around the melody and using the shuffle bowing. Using the fourth finger as indicated in the second part will help the tune flow smoother and make the bowing easier than using the open E string. Another possibility for variation on the second part is to add double stops and alter the descending run.

Irish Washerwoman

This tune has a different feel from any tune we have studied so far. It is written in $\frac{6}{8}$, which means there are six divisions of the measure with the eighth note equaling one division. It should be played with two beats in each measure with three eighth notes equaling one beat. Hence the rhythm pattern is ♫♩♫♩ .

The first and fourth notes of the measure fall on the beat.

The fifth and sixth measures of the second part should be played with the second finger held on the G on the E string while moving to each of the other notes. This will make for smoother fiddling. Irish washerwoman is a typical Irish jig.

Roy Acuff

Zeke Dawson — fiddler with George Jones and Loretta Lynn

Flowers of Edinburgh

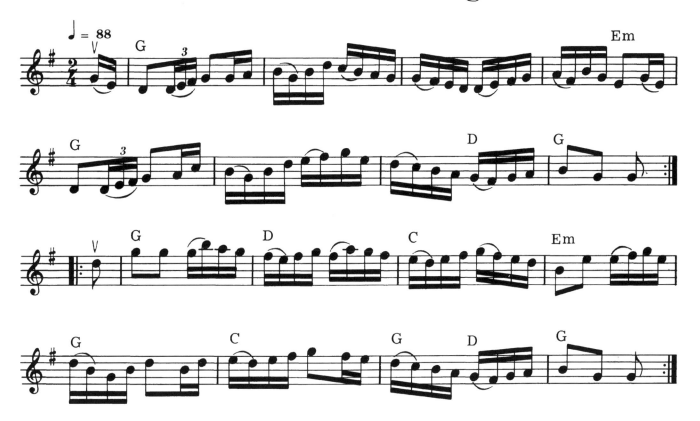

This is another type of Irish tune known as a reel. It can be embellished by adding triplets and trills. Here is an example of how this can be done.

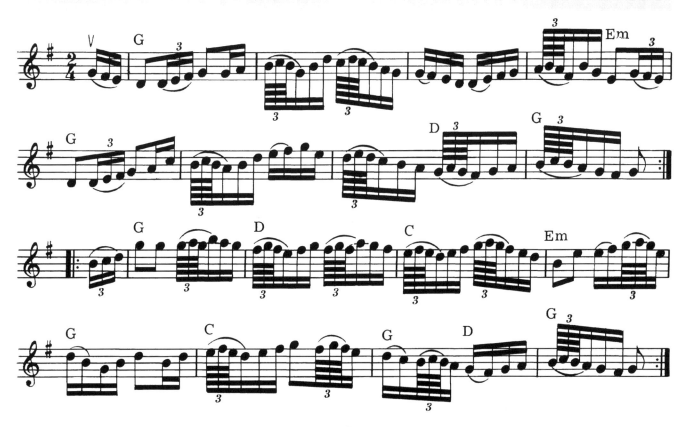

Blackberry Blossom

This melody provides an excellent theme for variation. Here are a few ways this can be done:

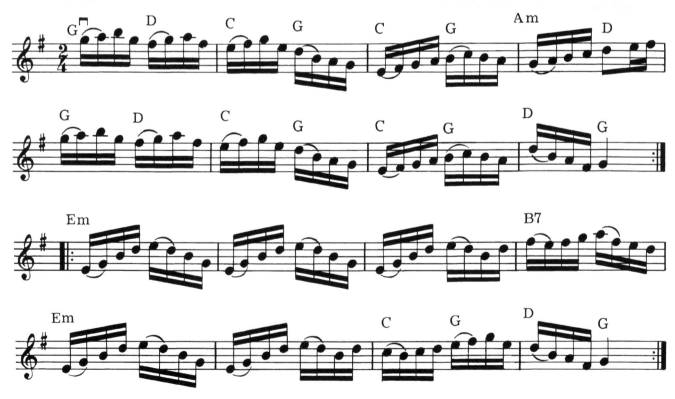

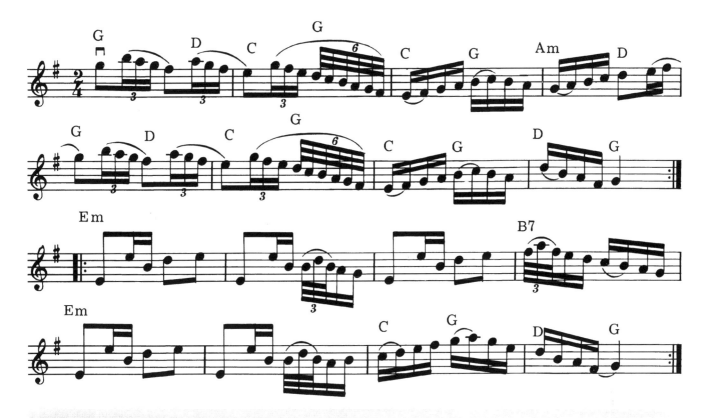

Measures 1-2 and 5-6 may also be varied in one of the following ways as well as by combining the variations presented previously.

Variation on measures 1-2, 5-6   Example of combination

Further examples of combination

Another possibility for the first part is to play it down an octave. The variations on measures 1-2 and 5-6 just presented will also apply to the lower octave.

61

Double Stops

The use of double stops is very common in fiddle practice. Often in the past, fiddlers played alone and had to furnish their own harmonies. Using double stops not only increased the harmonic interest of a tune, but also enabled the fiddlers to play louder. This was very important in the days before modern amplification. As fiddle music has developed to the present, double stops have remained an integral part.

The following two tunes are presented with a single melodic line and then with double stops. The double stop versions incorporate drones as well as harmonies moving with the melodies. Special care should be given to the fingerings and all accidentals that occur.

Bully of the Town

Pay particular attention to the pick up lick in the second ending of the first part and the first ending of the second part. This is a very common lick which is done by playing the triplet with very short, fast motions using the wrist, and then using two short up-bows on the following notes, leaving space between each note.

Down Yonder

Take notice of the coda sign in measure 12. On the repeat of the tune, play down to the sign, skip to the coda (measures 25-29), and complete the tune. On each repeat of the entire tune the same procedure is followed. Measures 13-16 are an embellishment of measures 9-12. These measures may be substituted for each other. There is a break in the back-up rhythm in the two measures in parentheses (measures 23-24). At this point, the fiddle may play the line in parentheses or it may be done by another instrument. The following arrangement of Down Yonder features the use of double stops. Special care should be given so that each double stop is played in tune.

Down Yonder — Double Stops

Key of C

The key of C has no flats or sharps. It is notated at the beginning
of the staff by the absence of flats and sharps like this:

There are three finger patterns used in the Key of C; one for the G string,
one for the D and A strings, and one for the E string. The pattern on
the G string has a whole step from open G to first finger, a whole step
from first to second finger, a half step from second to third finger,
with the fingers touching, and a whole step from third to fourth finger.
It looks like this:

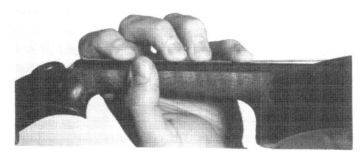

The pattern on the D and A strings has the second finger moved
back a half step to touch the first finger. It looks like this:

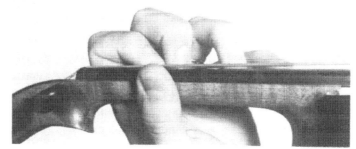

The finger pattern on the E string is different from any we have
studied so far. The first finger is played against the nut, a half
step from the open string. The remainder of the fingers are a whole
step apart. The low first finger should be played by extending the
finger backward rather than by moving the entire hand.

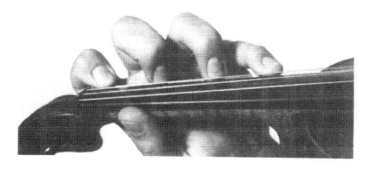

Here is a diagram of the notes in the key of C:

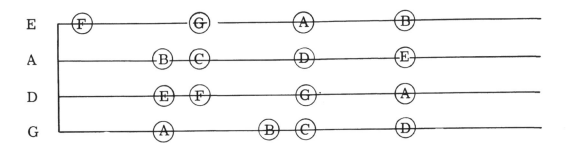

The corresponding notes on the staff are written like this:

Howdy Forrester

Swing Style

Many fiddle tunes are played in a swing style. In this style, the rhythm is slightly altered. Instead of playing consecutive eighth notes with exact evenness, they are played as quarter note eighth note triplets. Therefore  . As a general rule, a swing tune is played at a moderate tempo. This allows the tune to have a good strong bounce to it and the swing feel to stand out clearly.

Jimmy Mattingly

Stone's Rag

Stone's Rag is a good example of an old-time fiddle tune played in the swing style. The sixteenth notes written here are to be played in the manner just described. The tune is also known as the Lone Star Rag.

I Don't Love Nobody

    I don't Love Nobody is another good example of a fiddle tune which is to be played at a moderate tempo in the swing style. The fourth finger slides in measures 2, 6 and 10 are to be played in a bluesy manner. Likewise, the E's in measures 3 and 11 should be given the same feel.

Benny Martin

70

Billy in the Lowground

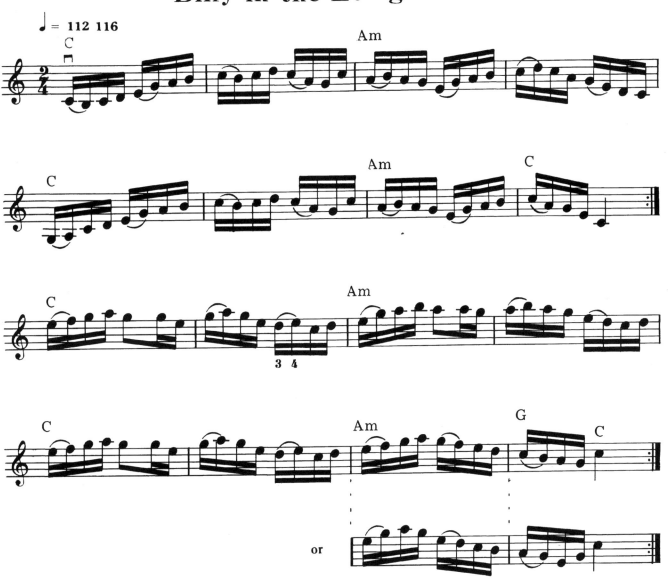

This is one of the more popular tunes and is played quite often at fiddle contests. Many fiddlers have their own versions and arrangements of Billy in the Lowground. You will notice two sets of endings for the second part. These are just two possibilities. Remember that fiddle tunes are not always played note for note the same way. The same fiddler may even play a tune differently each time he plays it, depending on his mood, how well he is playing that day, what comes into his thoughts and various other reasons.

East Tennessee Blues

This is a good breakdown in the key of C. It is based on an arrangement by Al Lester, a fiddler who has been state champion in both Virginia and Alabama. The tune will be easier to play if the suggested fourth fingers are used. By using the fourth finger instead of the open string in these places, a string crossing is eliminated and the bowing is smoother. The chords written in parenthesis are also commonly used with this tune.

Cross Shuffle
or
Double Shuffle

The cross shuffle is a bowing pattern found in many show tunes. It is also incorporated into back-up fiddling by many fiddlers. The pattern is sixteen notes long and consists of five groups of three notes plus one additional note. It is played on two or more strings and is achieved by crossing over to the next higher string for the third note of each group. The final note is played on the lower string. Thus the pattern looks like this:

Begin by practicing the cross shuffle slowly on two strings and work your speed up only after you are able to play it cleanly. The most common variation on the shuffle is to change the higher note on each crossing. In the key of C, a common way for this to be done is as follows:

It is also common to add the seventh (in this case, the B♭).

Tennessee Wagoneer

This is one of the more popular old-time fiddle tunes. It is presented here with a high and a low part, and a cross shuffle variation. The parts are based on various renditions heard both on stage and backstage at the Grand Ole Opry as well as other transcribed versions of the tune.

Back Up and Push

Back Up and Push is one of the well-known fiddle tunes done by country fiddlers. It is played in a bluesy manner with the use of slides. Both a single string version and a double stop version are presented here. The cross shuffle should be learned very accurately as written in the single string version and then expanded for the double stop version, as it is one of the most recognizable features of the piece.

Back Up and Push

Waltzes

The way a fiddler plays a waltz is often used as a judge of what kind of fiddler he is. A good fiddler uses long bow strokes and plays very smoothly when performing a waltz. The notes should flow from the instrument, never sounding forced by excess bow pressure. The pressure should remain consistent throughout the stroke and the bow must move at a right angle across the strings.

The following waltzes are a cross section of waltzes in the keys of A, D, G and C. They range from a clean and simple melodic line to complex double stops and embellishments. The turns, trills and double stops presented are characteristic of the style in which fiddle waltzes are performed and may be incorporated in a number of other waltzes.

Sweet Bunch of Daisies

Sweet Bunch of Daisies is an old-time fiddle waltz which is occasionally done in swing style. The version here is based upon Chubby Wise's version found on Stoneway Record number 104.

Rose of Sharon

This waltz should be played with long bow strokes to make each note sing as much as possible. The first part, which ends at bar 16, may be played down an octave.

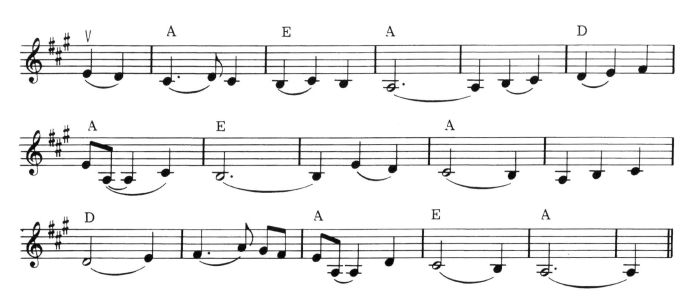

Westphalia Waltz

This is a simple version of Westphalia Waltz presenting a very straightforward melody. It is possible that a fiddler would play the melody like this, but more often he would embellish it with passing tones, double stops and other ornamentation. The following is an example of how these can be incorporated into the tune.

Westphalia Waltz

Over the Waves

This is the simple melody to Over the Waves, which is one of the most popular fiddle waltzes. The full length of the bow should be used so that a smooth, full sound comes from the fiddle. Be certain to keep the bow moving straight across the strings, allowing the speed and weight of the bow to produce the sound rather than pressing down hard with the right hand or arm. The A#'s and E#'s in measures 2, 12, 13, 18, 41 and 45 should be played with the first finger all the way up where the low second finger is normally placed.

Over the Waves

This arrangement is based on Kenny Baker's recording on County Record 719. The embellishments found here are very typical of waltz style fiddling. The upper neighboring tones found with the long notes, such as in measures 23-24, 31-32, 39-40, 47-48, 55-56 and 63-64 are characteristic of the way a long tone is embellished in all phases of fiddling.

Golden Anniversary Waltz

This waltz begins with a very common melodic line found in fiddle waltzes; that is, the first three notes of the melody descend from the key note (D - C♯ - B). The bowing should be done with long bow strokes using even pressure on both strings of the double stops. The trills are notated here as triplets, but the rhythm may be slightly varied or the trill omitted, and the melody will still be present. The double stops in measure 21 are to be played in third position using a slide to play the E♯ and G♯ as indicated. The A in measure 22 should be played open with the hand remaining in third position for the B and D on the next beat. Once again, in measure 25, the double stops are in third position. The C♯ is to be played by sliding the first finger back while maintaining position with the third finger on the B.

Golden Anniversary Waltz

This variation includes many trills and turns which are typical of the fiddle waltz style. The lick in measure 11 should be played with a short bow stroke, almost jerking, and then followed by a smooth trill. Measures 31 and 32 are typical of a waltz ending. When used as an ending they should be played with a broad bow stroke and ritarded (slowed down).

Frazier's Waltz

This waltz is based upon a rendition by Frazier Moss. As is common in fiddle waltzes, the tune is played through in one key - here the key of D, then transposed to another key - here the key of G, and then played again in its entirety in the original key. The fingerings are marked so that the double stops may be properly understood. There is constant shifting between first and third positions. This should be done smoothly, allowing only enough slide to phrase the notes in the fiddle style. Pay particular attention to all accidentals.

Additional

Favorites

Ramona Jones

Uncle Jimmy Thompson

*Photographs courtesy of the Country Music
Foundation Library and Media Center,
Nashville, Tennessee*

*Wilma Lee Cooper and the Clinch Mountain Clan
From left: Craig Duncan, Gene Wooten, Wilma Lee,
Terry Smith and Stan Brown*

Fire on the Mountain

This tune got its name from the speed at which it is played. It is usually done so fast that the fiddle seems to be "on fire," or that the fiddler must be "going to a fire." It can also be played with drones, giving it a fuller sound. The basic theme is only four measures long and is then repeated. The second part is in the key of D and is presented here as a variation on the theme, although an exact transposition of the original theme is also correct.

Red Haired Boy

This Scotch-Irish tune may be played many ways. It is presented here with a different bowing style than we have covered previously. The bow should change directions every half beat, thus giving a lilt to the tune. The tune may also be played by adding drones and creating the bagpipe sound.

Red Haired Boy
(With Drones)

Another possible way to play the tune is to use a dotted rhythm which is very characteristic of Scotch-Irish music. Two sixteenths would be replaced by a dotted sixteenth thirty-second ( ), and would be played with a slight space

or separation between each note. This is usually done at a slower tempo.

Cotton Eyed Joe

It is a common occurence for one name to be used for more than one fiddle tune. Such is the case with Cotton Eyed Joe. The first tune presented here is more common in Texas and the West. It is used for dances such as the two-step. This is a rather straightforward rendition using a drone E string. The third and fourth parts are merely variations on the first two parts. In the next to the last measure of the fourth part, the fourth finger is to stretch up for the C and then slide down for the B.

The second tune presented here is more common in the Appalachian Mountains and the Southeast. It is to be played faster than the other Cotton Eyed Joe and is often accompanied by singing. It is also a two part tune presented with a variation on each of the parts.

Cotton Eyed Joe

Ragtime Annie or Raggedy Ann

The first three measures of this tune should be played by rocking the bow from the A to the D string while remaining in contact with both strings. The "x's" in the example below indicate that the bow should still be in contact with that string although the emphasis is on the other string.

Example

The third finger G♮ in measures 4-6 should be played low with the second finger C♯ high, almost to the point of the second being under the third. The G is sounding as the seventh of the A chord. The second part is not repeated. Pay special attention to the slides in measures 19-21 and follow the fingerings indicated.

Pizzicato

Playing the fiddle with the fingers instead of using the bow is called pizzicato. One part of Champagne Polka is to be played by pulling or "plucking" the strings with the right index finger. This should be done over the fingerboard as illustrated.

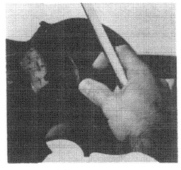

By playing over the fingerboard, the rosin on the strings is avoided and a fuller sound is obtained. The word "arco" means to play with the bow and usually follows a pizzicato section.

Champagne Polka is a two part tune with variations. It is presented here with the pizzicato variation and an embellished version incorporating the cross shuffle.

Champagne Polka

Cacklin' Hen

Variations on the second part

This tune is the fiddler's imitation of a cackling hen. It is generally played rather fast and incorporates many slides. The slide in the third measure should be done with the fourth finger beginning on B♭. The first finger slide in the first and second endings should start slightly below the pitch, move up and then move down, with the downward slide lasting longer than the upward slide. The first section should be played with long, full bow strokes. In contrast, the second part is to be played with shorter strokes. The E in measures 11 and 13 should be played with the fourth finger and should be accented. This part of the tune is imitating the hen. The variations of the second part are even further imitations of the hen cackling and should be played with this in mind. The first variation contains an extra measure which is typical of this style of fiddling. The G -F♮ - E figure in measures 16 and 17 should be exaggerated by use of a slide on the F♮. The second variation has seven consecutive G's which are to be played up-bow, stopping and jerking the bow between each note. The next slide is to be over exaggerated and drawn out. On the repeat of the lick, the bowing is slightly altered out of necessity, but the up-bows should still sound the same. The order of the tune is usually first part, second part, first part, second part, and variations of cackling. Sometimes the second part is also played in the key of D by moving across one string. The first part may return as an ending to the tune.

Maiden's Prayer

Var.2

Maiden's Prayer is presented here with a very straightforward melody and two variations characteristic of the fiddle style. The tune is to be played with a swing feel to it and is often done with a walking bass. Measures 1 and 9 are common variations on the rhythm of the opening. They may be interchanged, as both are correct representations of the melody. The eighth notes written throughout the tune are to be played with the swing style rhythm ♩♪♩♪ rather than even eighth notes.

The high E in the ending of the two variations should be played as a harmonic by extending the fourth finger and lightly touching the string halfway between the nut and the bridge. One common variation of Maiden's Prayer is to use tremolo bowing. This is done by rapidly moving the bow back and forth, out of rhythm, while sustaining a note with the left hand. It is best done in the upper half of the bow. The tremolo bowing can be made very effective by playing the notes of the second variation with the left hand, while using the tremolo with the right hand.

Katy Hill

Katy Hill is a tune from the South which is often played by bluegrass fiddlers. It is usually done quite fast with a driving tempo. Another tune very similar to Katy Hill and often confused with it is Sally Johnson. It comes from the Midwest and is usually played slower than Katy Hill, with more of a swing or bounce to the tempo. The major difference in the tunes is the E minor chord in measure 4 of Sally Johnson which is not present in Katy Hill. Also, Sally Johnson is usually played with many more variations than Katy Hill.

The Georiga shuffle has been used in the following arrangement of Sally Johnson. It is another bowing pattern known among fiddlers which is used thruoghout contest style fiddling as well as other styles. The name Georgia is somewhat misleading in that the pattern is used throughout many parts of the country. This pattern places the accent on the offbeat by playing down-bow on the offbeat and slurring the sixteenths between the offbeats with an up-bow.

Ex.

Special care should be given to the bow markings as this pattern is approached and left. As is usual, the Georgia shuffle is not used continuously throughout a tune, but is interspersed with other bowings so that the offbeat accents do not become monotonous.

Sally Johnson

Bill Cheatham

This is one of the more popular breakdowns played among bluegrass pickers. It is presented here with a straightforward melody using double stops and the shuffle bowing. Another possibility is to use single string sixteenth notes for the entire first part.

Bill Cheatham-Variation

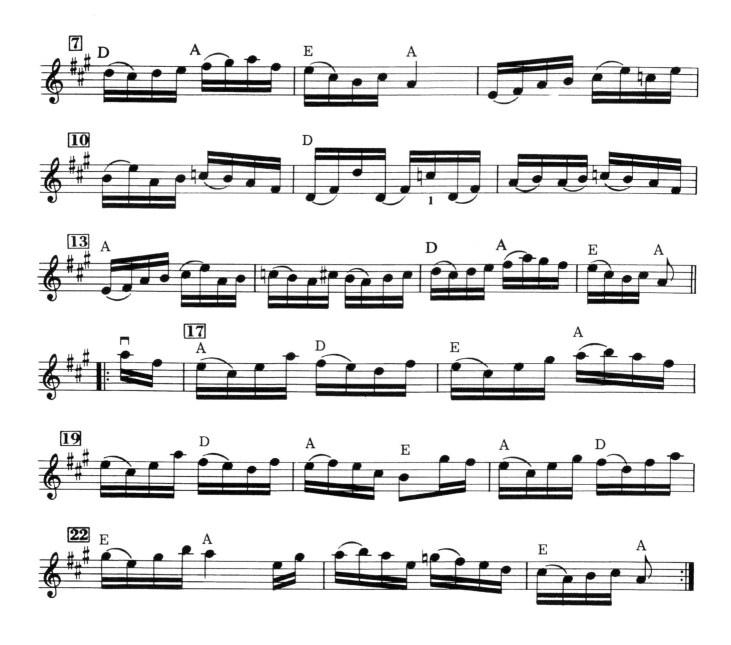

Notice the repeat of the first part is written out as another variation. It involves a chromatic lick in which the second finger makes a distinction between C♮ and C♯. The C♮ in measure 11 of the variation should be played with first finger because of the F♯ preceeding it. A variation on the second part is also presented. Even within this eight bar section two possibilities of playing the A - D - E - A chord change are presented. (Contrast measures 17 and 18 with measures 21 and 22). Variations on repetitions of tunes are very common in fiddling practice. Each tune a fiddler plays should be experimented with to determine new variations and phrasings. The bowing may be changed to create a new effect by using other patterns or combinations of patterns such as or the Georigia shuffle.

Made in the USA
Middletown, DE
21 August 2024

59523687R00060